EXPLORING ENERGY

WIND AND WATER POWER

PHILIP SAUVAIN

Editorial planning
Deborah Tyler

 SCHOOLHOUSE PRESS

Photographic credits

t = top b = bottom l = left r = right

cover: ZEFA; Chris Fairclough Picture Library

5 Alex Williams/Seaphot; 9 Frank Lane Picture Library;
10, 11, 12, ZEFA; 14 Mansell Collection; 15*t* ZEFA;
15*b* The National Trust; 17 ZEFA; 18*t* South American
Pictures; 18*b*, 21*t* ZEFA; 21*b* South American Pictures;
22 Peter Stevenson/Seaphot; 23 British Columbian
Embassy; 29*t* Chris Fairclough Picture Library; 29*b*,
31 ZEFA; 33 Central Electricity Generating Board;
34*t* Chris Fairclough Picture Library; 34*b* South American
Pictures; 35 David Redfern/Seaphot; 36 South American
Pictures; 37, 38 ZEFA; 39, 40 Science Photo Library;
41 Chris Fairclough Picture Library; 42 Frank Lane
Picture Agency; 43 Japan Ship Company; 44*t*, 44*b* ZEFA

Note to the reader
In this book there are some words in the text which are printed in **bold** type. This shows that the word is listed in the glossary on page 46. The glossary gives a brief explanation of words which may be new to you.

Contents

Introduction

Energy gives us heat and light. It makes us move. It moves machines. It makes all things, even plants and the sea, grow or move. We cannot see or feel this energy, but we can see the work it does. We need energy in order to live.

Energy is Work

Scientists used a Greek word "energeia," or "work," when they first thought about what makes things move. In time, "energeia" became our word "energy." Energy makes things do work. Work also makes other things move. Movement makes heat, and heat can make other things work. Energy always changes into some other type of energy when it is used. It is never lost or destroyed.

You may think that we can make energy, such as electricity. In fact, electricity is always made from other kinds of energy. These kinds of energy come from fast rivers, the wind, the waves, gas, oil, and coal. The only kind of energy we truly make is our own personal energy. We make our energy from the food we eat.

▶ Windsurfers use the energy of both wind and water. When wind fills the sail, the board moves faster through the water.

▼ Wind power and water power will provide the world with energy long after all the world's coal, oil, and natural gas has been burned.

Uses of energy throughout the world

Types of Energy

Scientists say that there are two major kinds of energy. The first kind of energy is stored in coal, in food, in lakes and rivers, or in the sun. This energy is ready for use. We call it **potential energy**. We store potential energy when we eat a meal or fill a car with gasoline. When this energy is being used, it is called **kinetic energy**. Kinetic energy is the second main type of energy. We are using kinetic energy when we run. When a river carries a boat down to the sea or turns a water wheel, it is using kinetic energy, too.

Using Energy

Some people use much more of the world's energy than others. They live in countries where there are many industries. They use energy to run machines in factories and hospitals and to light streets and buildings. They also use energy to heat homes and to move cars, trains, and planes.

People use several different kinds of energy. We use electrical energy to heat homes, light streetlights, and make machines run. **Electrical energy** is the easiest kind of energy to use. It can be turned on with the flick of a switch. Another kind of energy comes from **chemical** changes. The substances, or chemicals, in a battery make electricity so you can get light when you turn on a flashlight. **Chemical energy** also makes heat when we burn coal.

The power stored in the metal called uranium produces **nuclear energy** in nuclear power plants. Some people use the sun's rays to heat panels attached to the roofs of their homes. These solar panels heat their water. This is called **solar energy**.

Energy around Us

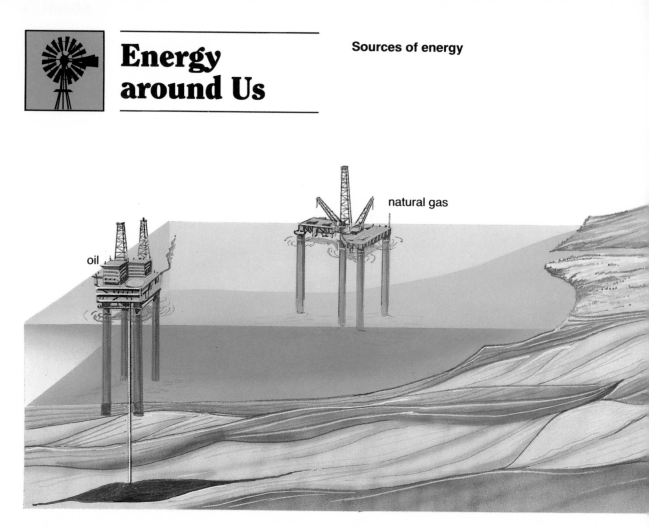

oil

natural gas

The sun supplies the earth with all of its energy. Energy is all around us. It is stored in the things we see each day. The sun's energy helps plants to grow. It makes rain. It causes winds. Lakes, rivers, and the oceans store the sun's energy in water. Trees store the sun's energy in wood. Trees, plants, and animals stored some of the sun's energy millions of years ago. Their remains rotted, and over time formed into coal, oil, and **natural gas**.

The Sun's Heat

Over five billion years ago the earth was a ball of boiling liquid rock. There is still a lake of liquid rock boiling deep below the earth's surface. The heat from the boiling, liquid rock makes hot water under the ground. There are hot springs at Yellowstone National Park in Wyoming. The hot water from under the earth's surface is also used to heat buildings in New Zealand, Italy, and Iceland. This heat from the liquid rock inside the earth is called **geothermal energy**.

Winds and Water

Energy from the sun heats the land on the earth during the day. The heat from the land warms the air above. Warm air rises because it is lighter than cold air. Cold air sinks. So, the air above the hot lands at the **equator** is always rising. Air from colder lands moves in to take its

6

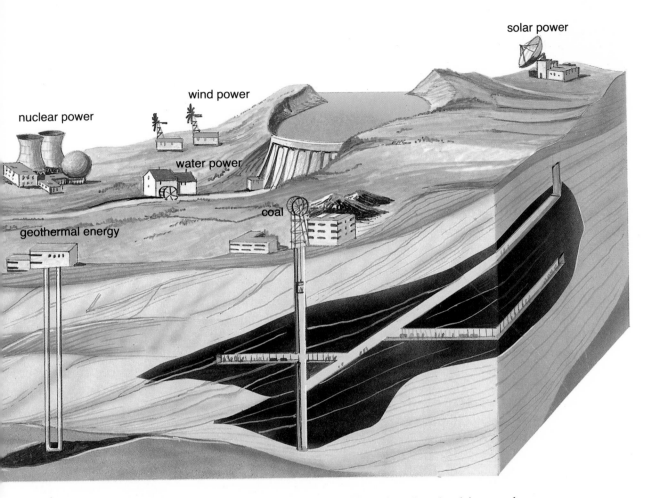

solar power

wind power

nuclear power

water power

geothermal energy

coal

place. This movement of air from cold to hot lands and from hot to cold lands produces **wind currents**.

The sun also heats the surface of the earth's oceans. Winds and the way the earth turns keep the oceans moving. Some of the warmer water moves toward the cold seas. Colder water moves toward the warm seas. These movements of water are called **ocean currents**.

Weather

The sun's heat turns water from the sea into tiny droplets which collect in the air to form **water vapor**. The vapor forms clouds. The same thing happens when a wet bathing suit dries in the sun. The

water in the bathing suit turns to water vapor. It **evaporates**. The water vapor in the clouds falls back to the earth in the form of rain. Rain falls into lakes and rivers, and the water returns to the sea.

Using Wind and Water Energy

Wind and water have been used as sources of energy for thousands of years. People are now trying to find new ways of using wind power and water power. There are two good reasons for this recent interest. There will always be winds. There will always be water. This is because they are replaced, or renewed, by the sun. We call wind and water power **renewable** sources of energy.

Winds

The air around the earth is called its **atmosphere**. It is divided into three main layers. The lowest layer is called the **troposphere**. It is about eight miles high. Our weather is formed there. In this layer, the air is always moving. Gases in the layer above press down on the air in the troposphere. This weight is called **air pressure**.

Wind Patterns

Warm air is lighter than cold air. Air pressure is lower at the equator because the weather is hot there. Air pressure is higher at the North and South Poles because the weather is cold there. Cold air is heavier than warm air. These areas of **high pressure** and **low pressure** influence our weather. The warm air at the equator rises into the higher levels of the troposphere.

Cooler air from the North and South Poles moves in over the land to take its place. As the cooler air is heated by the sun, it also rises and again, more cool air moves in. The air in the troposphere is always moving. The movement causes winds. The winds blow in the same direction for much of the year. You can see these wind patterns on the map.

The direction of the wind depends, for the most part, on the way the earth turns. The turning movement of the earth is called **rotation**. Winds blowing south from the North Pole to the equator swing around to the right because of the rotation of the earth. If you live between the Tropic of Cancer and the equator, the winds usually blow from the northeast. Southeast winds blow from the Tropic of Capricorn to the equator. Sailors learned these wind patterns. They called them the Trade Winds and established trade routes that took advantage of these wind patterns.

▼ Hot air rises. Then, cold air takes its place. The cold air also heats up and rises. The flow of air continues to go around and around.

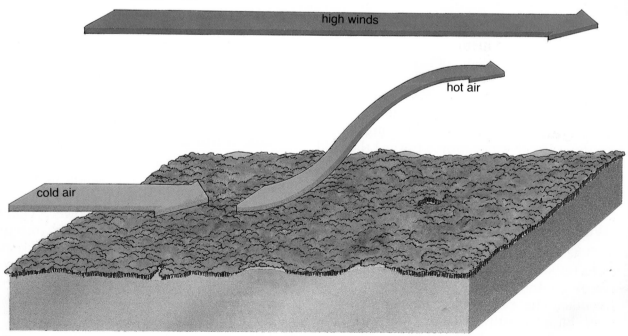

high winds

hot air

cold air

NORTH AMERICA

EUROPE

ASIA

China

Tropic of Cancer

AFRICA

India

equator

SOUTH AMERICA

AUSTRALASIA

Tropic of Capricorn

▲ Knowing about the winds was very important in the days of the sailing ship. Skillful use of the Trade Winds helped sailors to take goods to many different countries. Wool, tin, and wood came from the northern countries, and silks and spices came from China and India – all in ships powered by the Trade Winds.

▼ You can feel the power of the wind in a storm. The storms with the strongest winds are called hurricanes. A hurricane caused this damage to property in Houston, Texas.

The Power of the Wind

In the days before ships had engines, all large ships had sails. The ships used the power of the wind to take them from port to port. The first sea traders we know about were sailors from Egypt. About 12,000 years ago, they figured out how to use the winds' power and patterns to move sailing boats.

People found another way of using the wind when they built windmills. The wind's power moved the windmill's sails around, and made the **millstones** turn. Today, we use wind power to make electricity. Using the wind as a source of power has many advantages. The wind is free. It is almost always there. It can be used during most of the year.

Windmills

The first farmers worked very hard to grow food. They dug up the ground, sowed seeds, and harvested their crops. They grew grain like wheat or corn. They rubbed the ears of corn between large, flat stones called millstones to make flour. Some of the farmers used animals to turn the millstones. Other people did all of their work by hand. They had no other source of power until the water wheel and the windmill were invented.

The First Windmills

About 1,300 years ago, the people of **Persia** in the Middle East began to use windmills. At first, the Persians used the windmills to lift water from rivers and wells. Later, the cloth sails were put inside buildings with long rooms. These rooms had narrow slits in the walls. When the wind blew through these slits in the walls, it turned the cloth sails.

The sails were attached to an upright, or

▲ People on the Greek island of Crete knew that the wind moved their sailing boats. They figured out that similar sails on a windmill would turn a wheel. Today, there are still windmills with boat sails being used in southern Europe.

vertical, pole. The end of this pole, or main **shaft**, turned a millstone on the floor above. Because the sails of this type of windmill turned around parallel with the floor like a helicopter's propeller, they are called **horizontal mills**.

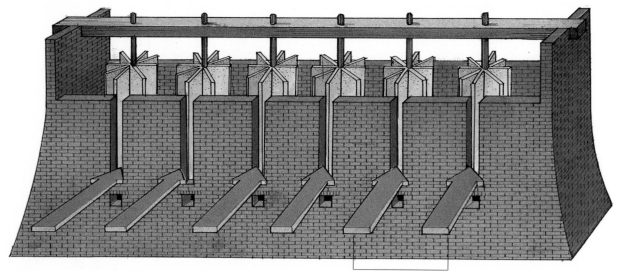

A horizontal windmill

wind

▲ This is the inside of an old wooden windmill. The heavy millstone on the right is turned by the gear wheel above it.

Windmills in Europe

About 800 years ago, people in Europe began to build wooden windmills. These windmills had long, narrow, canvas sails on the outside of the building. These sails turned at right angles to the ground instead of parallel with the ground. Windmills of this type are called **vertical mills**. The earliest vertical mill was called a **post mill**. The end of the main shaft was linked to wheels which turned the millstone. These mills were built on a thick, central post, so that the miller could turn the whole post mill to face into the wind. This was very hard work. In 1745, in Britain, Edmund Lee invented the fantail. It was a set of small blades, or **vanes**. The blades were attached to the main sails of the windmill at right angles. Millers were amazed to see that the fantail turned the windmill around by itself to face into the wind.

Taller windmills, called **tower mills** or **smock mills**, made efficient use of the fantail. They were first built about 500 years ago from brick or stone. They were built on hills so that they were able to use the stronger winds which blow higher above the ground. Only the cap of the tower mill, with its fantail and sails, turned to face the wind.

Using Windmills

People used windmills to grind ears of corn, to crush seeds, to grind chalk, and to saw wood. Five hundred years ago, the Dutch people started to drain the flooded parts of The Netherlands. They used energy from windmills to help them with this work. Windmills helped them pump the water away from the land.

Water Wheels

▼ The Asi River turns these huge water wheels at Hammah in Syria. The water wheels provide power for pumps which supply water to nearby houses.

Thousands of years ago, people figured out that running water had the power to move things. They felt this power when they waded through a river or had to swim across it.

The Romans

The horizontal wheel was the simplest type of Roman water wheel. It had paddles attached to a vertical shaft. These were spun around by a fast-flowing stream or river. The shaft then turned a grindstone inside the building that was built above the stream.

The Romans also used vertical water wheels. A Roman engineer named Marcus Vitruvius Pollio wrote about these water wheels 2,000 years ago. This is why vertical water wheels are sometimes called Vitruvian wheels.

Kinds of Water Wheels

There are three common kinds of water wheel. When the water in a river pushes a wheel from below, the wheel is called an **undershot** wheel. The water shoots under the wheel. Undershot wheels are suitable for use on slow rivers, such as those rivers found in flat lands, near the sea.

Water shoots over the top of some wheels to make them spin. The **overshot** wheel works best in fast-flowing rivers. This is why they were often built in hilly areas where rivers ran downhill swiftly.

Wheels which turn when the water hits the blades in the middle of the wheel are called **breastshot** water wheels.

Water power was used to run all kinds of machinery. At first, water wheels were used to grind cereal crops. Later, they were used to make iron and steel in forges and to make cloth in mills. By 1800, there were half a million water mills in Europe. Some water mills are still working.

Bringing Water to the Mill

An overshot or breastshot water wheel had to have water flowing over it all the time in order to turn it. Narrow channels, called **aqueducts** or **leats**, took the water from the river to the water mill. The water flowed down a chute, called the **headrace**, to the water wheel. This flow was controlled by a special gate, called the **penstock**. Another channel, the **tailrace**, took the water back to the river after it had been used. In dry weather, the level of the rivers dropped. In order to keep the water flowing over the mill wheel, dams, or **weirs**, were built across the river. The water formed a millpond behind the dam. The water in the millpond was used when it was needed.

▼ The blades of undershot wheels dip into the water. The water falls onto the blades of overshot wheels. Falling and flowing water turn the breastshot wheel.

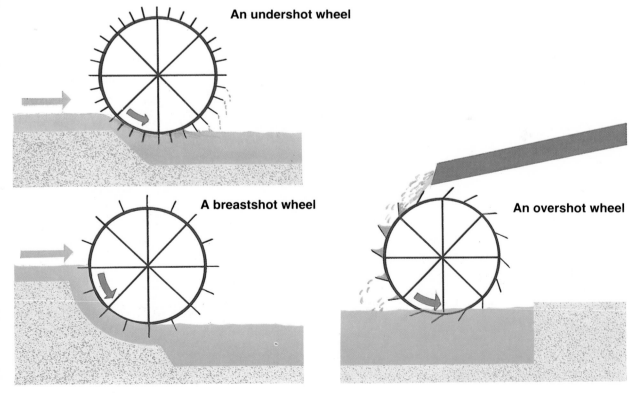

An undershot wheel

A breastshot wheel

An overshot wheel

Water Wheels for Industry

The first people on the earth lived in groups. They made their own shelters and grew their own food. They made their own tools. They were skilled at many jobs.

The First Machines

About 6,000 years ago, the workers in the first towns started to develop special skills. Some people made pots. Other people spun thread or wove cloth. These activities were the first **industries**. Much later on, people used their hands or feet to work simple machines, such as the spinning wheel.

Water Mills

Millers were probably the first people to use water power to run machines. They used them to turn the millstones which ground corn into flour. About 500 years ago, water wheels were used to crush chalk and rocks. Water wheels were also used to run machinery which squeezed oil out of olives. Woollen cloth could be cleaned by water power. The power came from the shaft of the water wheel as it turned. Blacksmiths used water power to lift the heavy hammers that they used to make iron tools.

▼ One mill can work for many people. Here, farmers are bringing sacks of grain to the water mill. The huge wheels under the mill turn the millstones. Two more water mills are working down in the river.

Ioan. Stradanus invent. Phls Galle excud.

▲ Water mills made it easier to do many jobs. An overshot wheel powers this 150-year-old sawmill in the forests of New Brunswick, Canada. The energy of the water powers saws to cut the wood.

People and animals get tired when they do heavy work. A water wheel does not. The water wheel continues working as long as there is water to turn the wheel. Richard Arkwright used a water wheel to power the world's first cotton-spinning mill in Britain in 1771.

Mills and Rivers

Water power was cheap, but it did have problems. Water wheels worked slowly. Also, they could turn only a few machines at the same time. In dry weather, the level of the water in the pond dropped. Mud and weeds choked up the millpond. The millpond and the millstream had to be cleaned out periodically.

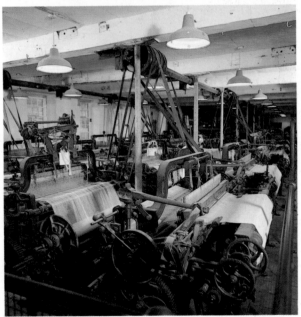

▲ The power for these weaving machines comes from a huge water wheel. The wheel turns the iron shaft on the roof. The belts take the power to the weaving machines.

15

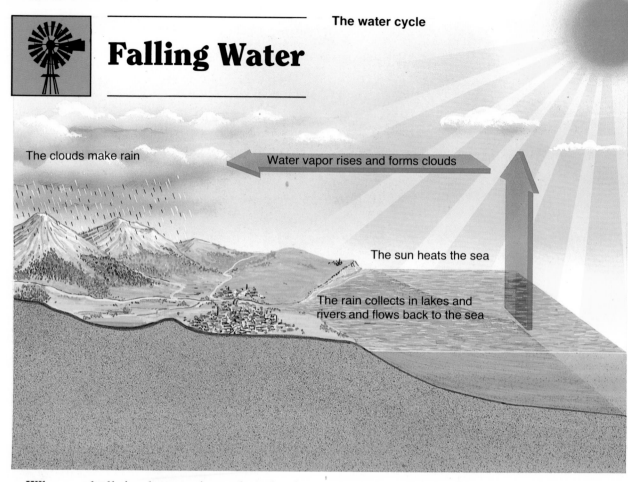

Falling Water

The clouds make rain

Water vapor rises and forms clouds

The sun heats the sea

The rain collects in lakes and rivers and flows back to the sea

When a ball is thrown into the air, it falls back to the ground. It does not go on and on, up into the sky. The power which pulls the ball back to the earth is called the **force of gravity**. Gravity pulls everything downward, including rain, rivers, and falling water.

Moving Water

Water is always on the move. It travels in a repeated pattern called the **water cycle**. The cycle begins when the sun heats the sea. Heat causes water to rise up into the air in the form of water vapor.

The warm water vapor forms clouds. These clouds cool when they rise over hills or pass over land. When the clouds get colder, they are unable to hold all their water. The force of gravity makes the water in the clouds fall as rain, hail, or snow.

Then the rain or snow when it melts, runs into pools and small streams. The pools and streams grow into bigger rivers and run into lakes. The level of the sea is almost always lower than the land, so the force of gravity makes the water flow back toward the sea. Then the water cycle begins again.

The water cycle is how clouds, rain, and rivers store energy from the sun. The sun's energy lifts water from the seas and puts it into lakes and, especially, rivers. Today, we use the energy in rivers to produce electricity. We call this a **hydroelectric power** system. The word "hydro" comes from a Greek word, "hydor," meaning water.

Waterfalls

Have you ever watched a waterfall? If you have, you know how powerful a waterfall is. The energy is in the water all the time. Engineers have found out how to use the energy in the water when we need it most. This is through the use of hydroelectric power. Dams are built above waterfalls to hold back the water. This makes a lake, or **reservoir**. From there, the water flows down to a lower level through pipes. The energy in the water falling from the reservoir to the lower level is turned into electricity. We make hydroelectricity only when we need it, because we cannot store it. We can only store the water.

► You can see the power of falling water in this waterfall in Wyoming. The water has made a deep pool at the bottom of the Yellowstone Falls. The strong flow of water has cut a steep-sided valley through the rock.

Building Dams

A dam keeps water from flowing. The level of the water rises and spreads out behind the dam, where it forms a reservoir. The weight of this water presses against the dam wall. Engineers have to make sure the dam will be strong enough to stand up against this pressure. Water pouring down the valley from a break in a dam can destroy everything in its path. It can also drown people and animals.

Finding a Place to Build a Dam

Engineers have to search hard for a good place to build a dam. They look for a river which will keep the reservoir filled up, even in dry weather. They look for a deep, narrow valley where the river falls steeply. There is more power in water which falls steeply. The height from which the water falls from the reservoir to the power plant is called the **head of water**. Also, engineers need less earth, rock, and concrete to build a dam across a narrow valley. Dams are very expensive to build.

▲ The Paraná River forms the border between Brazil and Paraguay in South America. The land is flat, but both countries needed electricity. The Itaipu Dam now supplies both countries with electricity.

◀ The Itaipu Dam is nearly finished here. A large area behind the dam has been flooded to make a reservoir. Water is flowing down the spillway.

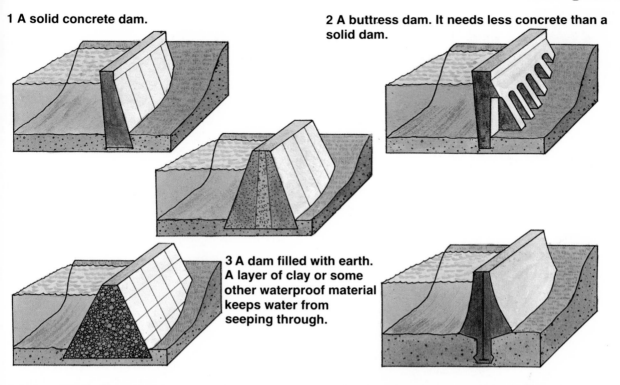

1 A solid concrete dam.

2 A buttress dam. It needs less concrete than a solid dam.

3 A dam filled with earth. A layer of clay or some other waterproof material keeps water from seeping through.

4 A dam filled with rocks or stones. It is lined with concrete or steel plates.

5 A dam with deep foundations made of steel.

Kinds of Dams

The kind of dam chosen for a valley depends partly on the rocks and earth found nearby because these rocks and earth may be used as building materials. Some dams are made of thick, solid concrete all the way across. These dams keep back the water just because they are so heavy. They slope backward at an angle.

Buttress dams also slope backward at an angle. However, they have huge, solid concrete supports, called buttresses, at the front. These buttresses strengthen the dam wall.

Many of the world's largest dams are made of earth, or rocks and stones. Dams filled with rocks and stones have a smooth outer surface, or skin, made of concrete or steelplating. Engineers strengthen some dams by sinking strong steel supports deep into the rocks below the ground.

Sometimes, there is too much water in the reservoir. When this happens, a **spillway** lets the water drain away to take the pressure off the dam.

Changes in the Land

Building a dam always changes the countryside. New roads are built. The roads are needed to bring machinery and materials to the dam site. Sometimes, a road runs right across the dam wall.

Because dams are often built in places which are far away from towns or villages, the workers who build the dams need somewhere to live. Houses or hotels are built for them. When a reservoir is to be formed behind a new dam, people living in the valley are moved to another area. Then, the water builds up behind the dam and fills the reservoir. Life in the valley is changed completely by a new dam.

The Need for More Power

At the beginning of the 1800s, the first factory owners soon found they had to have more power. They knew that the more goods they made, the more they would sell. Because a single water wheel could only power a few machines at the same time, they looked for ways of making extra power to run more machines. Some factory owners began to use a new type of water wheel called a **turbine**.

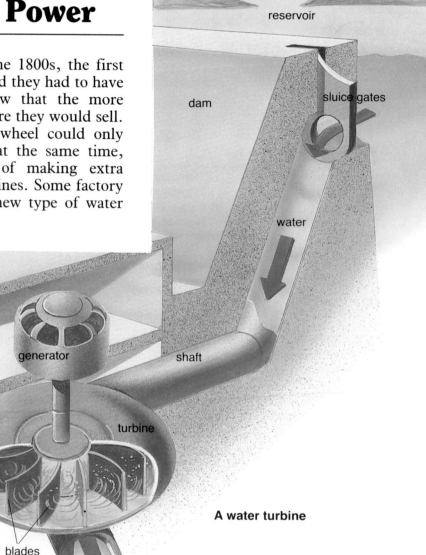

A water turbine

Water Turbines

Benoit Fourneyron invented the water turbine in France in 1827. He made falling water swirl around as it rushed down a pipe. The force of this spinning water turned the blades on a wheel. The machine was called a turbine after "turbo," the Latin word for a whirlwind. Factories first used turbines about 150 years ago.

The water turbine made it possible to make hydroelectricity from running water. Water passes through an opening in the dam wall controlled by **sluice gates**. It falls steeply down tubes to the penstock which feeds water to the turbine. The force of the water makes the turbine spin rapidly. The turbine drives a machine which makes electricity.

◀ Wind turbines are still an unusual sight in the countryside. They can be used to make electricity for people's homes.

Wind Turbines

The windmill was a simple type of turbine. It moved very much like a water turbine, but in slow-motion. Today, wind generators spin very rapidly. They have streamlined vanes, blades, or propellers. Wind generators like these only work when the wind speed is at least ten miles per hour.

There are two main kinds of wind turbine. Vertical turbines with a horizontal shaft have two or three blades. They spin very fast, like the propellers on a plane. Horizontal wind turbines look like giant eggbeaters. They spin around on an upright shaft. The turbines can use the wind when it blows from any direction.

▶ Inside the power plant beneath the Itaipu Dam. The water turbines began to generate electricity in 1985. They will work at full power in 1990.

Water Power

Falling water turns turbines which make, or **generate**, electricity from water power. Hydroelectric power systems make about a quarter of the world's electricity. They use a renewable source of energy. Rain fills up the lakes and rivers again with the water which supplies the power.

Water from the Mountains

Many hydroelectric power systems are built in the hills or mountains where there are waterfalls and fast-flowing rivers. Heavy rainfall keeps the rivers filled with water. The main disadvantage is that only a few people live in the mountains. Most of the world's hydroelectricity has to be brought to distant towns and factories. Tasmania makes one tenth of the electricity Australia uses. Yet only one twentieth of the people of Australia live in Tasmania. However, some hydroelectric systems have brought new industries to new towns built in the mountains.

▼ The Spokane River in the state of Washington is a good site to make hydroelectric power. This narrow dam is built against the rock of the valley sides. Water flows down the pipes at the sides into the power plant. The rate of flow of the river is controlled by the spillway.

▲ The Kitimat Project in Canada.

The Kitimat Project

Once only a few trappers and hunters lived in the Kitimat area in Canada. Today, Kitimat is a city of over 10,000 people. An aluminum company built the hydroelectric system and the town. They needed cheap electricity to make the aluminum.

First, engineers built a huge dam across the Nechako River. This is the Kenney Dam. It is built on a site about 155 miles from Kitimat. The dam forms a huge reservoir about the size of the state of Connecticut. The water in the dam falls 2,600 feet through a tunnel in Mount DuBose. Engineers built the Kemano Power Plant inside the mountain. The mountain helps to withstand the force of the falling water. The water turns the turbines which make electricity.

Tall steel towers, called **pylons**, carry cables which take the electricity from Kemano to Kitimat. These cables are called **power lines**. They cross the lonely Kildala Pass. This is why the project is sometimes called the "Four K project" – Kenney, Kemano, Kildala, and Kitimat.

Hydroelectric Systems

Hydroelectric power systems have been built all over the world. Most of them get their power from dams across rivers. Some systems are tiny. Others are huge. The Grande Dixence Dam in Switzerland is only 2,275 feet long but it is 926 feet high. The Kiev Dam in the USSR is only sixty-five feet high, but it is over thirty miles in length.

The biggest hydroelectric system in the world will soon be the earth-filled dam at Itaipu. This is on the Paraná River between Brazil and Paraguay in South America. Itaipu will produce six times as much electricity as a large power plant that burns coal.

▶ The orange areas of the map show which parts of the world produce the most hydroelectricity. In these areas, there are high mountains and long rivers. The chart shows how much hydroelectricty some countries use. The United States uses more hydroelectricity than any other country.

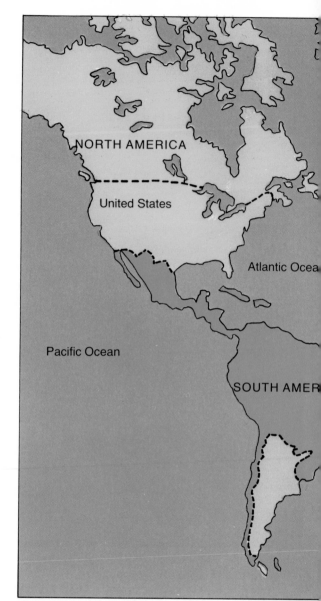

The Highest, Biggest, Longest Dams in the World

	Name of Dam	Country	Measurements	Type
Tallest dams	Rogun	USSR	1,089 ft high	rock
	Nourek	USSR	1,030 ft high	rock
	Grande Dixence	Switzerland	926 ft high	concrete
Largest dams	Tarbela	Pakistan	4.9 billion cubic ft	earth
	Fort Peck	US	3.36 billion cubic ft	earth

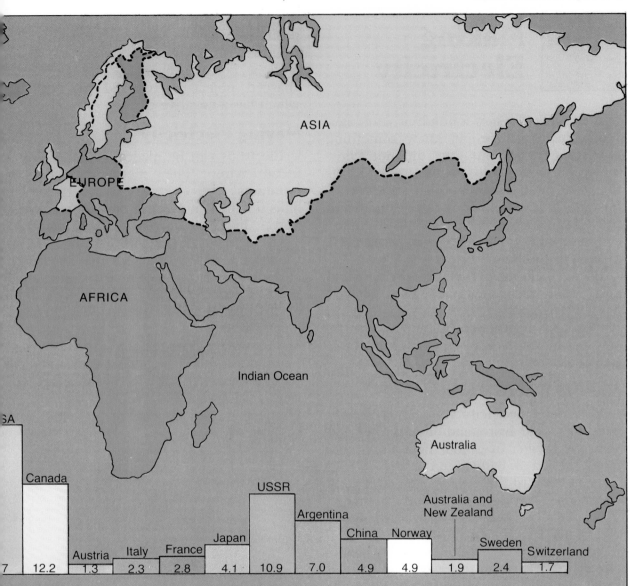

Map showing ASIA, EUROPE, AFRICA, Indian Ocean, Australia, with a bar chart of values:

USA	Canada	Austria	Italy	France	Japan	USSR	Argentina	China	Norway	Australia and New Zealand	Sweden	Switzerland
7	12.2	1.3	2.3	2.8	4.1	10.9	7.0	4.9	4.9	1.9	2.4	1.7

The Highest, Biggest, Longest Dams in the World

	Name of dam	Country	Measurements	Type
Longest dam	Yacryeta-Apipe	Argentina and Paraguay	45 miles long	earth
Largest reservoirs	Bratsk	USSR	106 cubic miles of water	earth
	Aswan High Dam	Egypt	103 cubic miles of water	earth
	Kariba	Zimbabwe	100 cubic miles of water	concrete
	Akosombo	Ghana	93 cubic miles of water	rock

Making Electricity

Electricity was new a hundred years ago. Until that time, people knew something about electricity, but they did not know what work it could do. Electricity has many advantages over other sources of energy. It is clean. It is always ready to use. Also, it can be made from many different types of energy – even **fossil fuels** such as oil and coal.

Fossil fuels cannot be renewed. Wind and water are renewable. This is why people have started to look again at wind power and water power. We need the electricity which wind power and water power can generate.

Making Electricity Yourself

You make electricity yourself. You may have seen your hair stand on end after you pulled a sweater over your head. You may have rubbed a balloon on a carpet and made it stick to the ceiling. The electricity which does this does not move. It remains still. This is why it is called **static electricity**.

Scientists have found out why static electricity behaves in this way. Today, they know that all things on the earth are made up of tiny atoms, about one billionth of an inch in width. Each of these atoms contains even tinier bits, or particles, of electricity. There are three kinds of particles but two kinds have electrical charges. They are **electrons** and **protons**. Most atoms hold equal numbers of these particles. Electrons have one type of electric force. We call it a negative electrical charge. Protons have a positive electrical charge. An object with a negative charge is attracted to an object with a positive charge. The negatively charged object is repelled by anything which has a negative charge.

Moving Electricity

Electrons can be made to move along a metal wire. The metal attracts, or **conducts**, the electrons along the wire. This is called an **electric current** because it moves like the current in a stream. In 1820, a Danish scientist named Hans Christian Öersted found out that an electric current running through an object could make that object attract other objects. The electric current could produce **magnetism**. Then, scientists tried to find out if a magnet could produce electricity. Michael Faraday showed them that it could. He pushed a magnet into a coil of wire and out again. By doing this over and over again, Faraday made an electric current pass along the wire.

▶ Rubbing a balloon takes away some of its positive electric charges. This is why the negative charges in the balloon stick to the positive electric charges on the ceiling.

▼ The ancient Greeks were the first to know about static electricity. When they rubbed a stone called amber with silk, they found out that the stone could then pick up dust and straw.

▼ A British scientist named William Gilbert used "elektron," a Greek word for amber, when he invented the word "electric" about 400 years ago. He used this new word to help him describe the way in which some objects are attracted to another object, such as iron filings to a magnet.

▲ In 1831, a British scientist named Michael Faraday showed that a magnet could produce electricity, if it was passed in and out of a coil of wire.

▲ In 1881, an American inventor named Thomas Alva Edison built an electricity generating plant. It supplied electric power to people in the city of New York. This was the world's first public electricity service.

The Big Power Plants

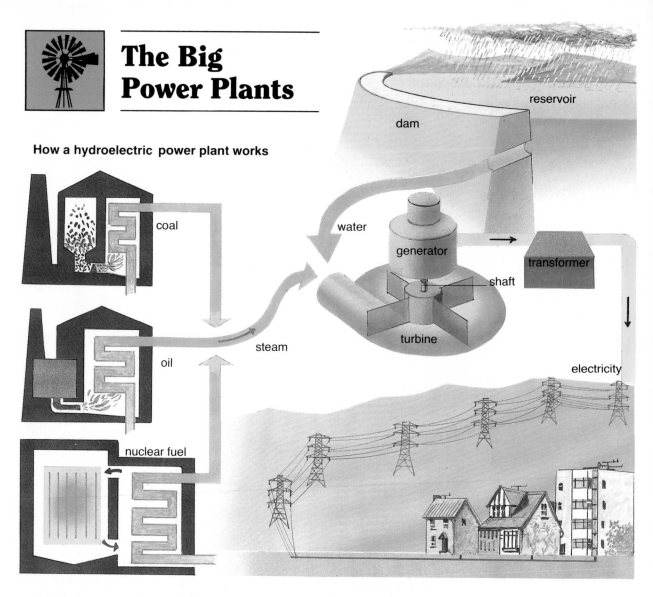

How a hydroelectric power plant works

coal

oil

nuclear fuel

water

steam

reservoir

dam

generator

shaft

transformer

turbine

electricity

Faraday's method of making electricity is still used in power plants today. When the turbines spin around at high speed, they turn an electromagnet inside a coil of wire. The movement generates an electric current. This is why it is called a **generator**.

Water turbines are run by water power in hydroelectric power systems. Other power plants burn fossil fuels, such as coal or oil, to make steam. Then, the steam is forced through a turbine. The steam spins the turbine blades. Nuclear power plants use the power in atoms to make electricity. This is called nuclear energy. The nuclear energy makes heat. The heat makes steam. The steam turns the turbines.

The electricity produced by these power plants is changed by a **transformer**, so it can be sent along the power lines. Sometimes, the power lines are put underground, so they do not spoil the countryside. The electricity is carried by the power lines to offices, hospitals, factories, and homes. It is used for heating, lighting, and to run machines.

► The control room in a power plant is worked by computers and automatic machines. Only a small number of people are needed to run a power plant.

► This dam makes up part of the Nurek hydroelectric scheme in the USSR. Fast-flowing water turns the turbines which make the electricity. Power lines carry the electricity away.

Supply and Demand

▶ Power lines are like rivers of electricity. They crisscross the land to take power to homes and factories. Many people think they spoil the beauty of the countryside.

Electricity is needed day and night throughout the year. The demand for electricity goes up each year. Schools, homes, hospitals, factories, and farms all make use of electricity in thousands of different ways.

Electricity is easy to use, but it cannot be stored for future use. You cannot buy it and store it before you use it, like coal or oil. People use much more electricity at some times than at others. Power plants have to be able to supply electricity whenever people demand it.

▼ In some parts of the world, the highest demand for electricity often occurs when a popular television program comes to an end on a cold winter's night. All at the same time, people in millions of homes turn on their stoves or coffee-makers to make a cup of coffee.

Supply

Power plants supply electricity by sending it along the power lines. Often, the power lines are linked together to form a power grid. The grid supplies power to a large number of homes and buildings.

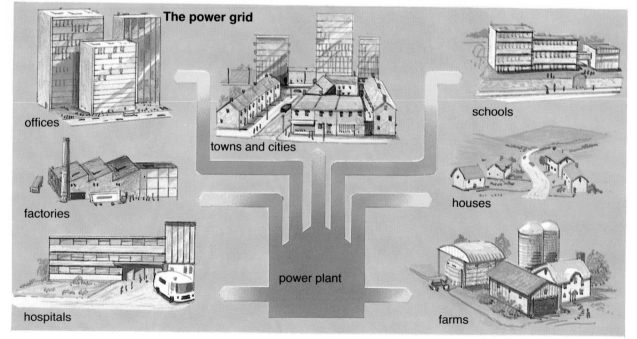

The power grid

offices

towns and cities

schools

factories

houses

hospitals

power plant

farms

The flow of electricity is measured in **volts**. This is like measuring the flow of water in a large river. The turbines in most power plants generate electricity at a pressure of about 25,000 volts before the electricity is sent along the power lines. The pressure is then lowered, so it can be used safely in homes and factories. Homes, schools, stores, and offices use electricity at a lower pressure than factories. Factories with large, powerful machines need electricity at a higher pressure.

Demand

People do not need the same amount of electricity all the time. The demand varies. It depends on where people are and what they are doing. Demand for electricity is usually at its highest in the early evening during the winter. That is the time when many people come home from school and work. They turn on the lights and the heat, and they may start to make dinner. They may turn on the television. They will need electricity for some or all of these things. Much less electricity is needed to meet people's demands on a warm day in the middle of the summer.

The lowest amount of electricity needed every day throughout the year is called the **base load**. The greatest amount of electricity needed at special times is called the **peak load**.

Coal, oil, and nuclear power plants generate electricity from steam. They make it cheaply when the turbines are running at top speed. It takes about eight hours to make the steam and start the turbines again if they have not been used for a while. This makes it hard to meet the demand for power if the weather turns very cold suddenly.

Hydroelectric power plants are easier to control. The water is always there. These plants can make electricity within two minutes. They can also increase the supply of electricity very quickly, when it is necessary.

Storing Energy

Oil can be stored in a tank until it is needed. We cannot do this with wind power or electricity. We have to change them into another kind of energy which we can store.

Wind Power

Windmills can be used to make electricity from wind power. They make the most electricity on very windy days. Engineers use the extra electricity made on windy days to pump water from a lake up to a higher lake. On calm days, the wind generator shuts down. Then, the water in the higher lake is allowed to fall to the lower level. The power of the falling water is used to make hydroelectricity. Wind generators can help to supply towns with electricity throughout the year.

Engineers can also use the extra electricity made on windy days to force, or compress, air into a tank. This **compressed air** can be stored until it is needed. It can be used on calm days to spin a turbine to generate electricity.

Using a wind generator to pump water

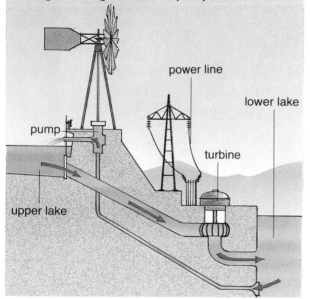

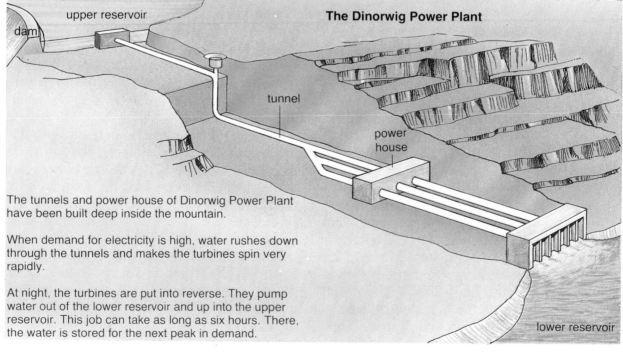

The Dinorwig Power Plant

The tunnels and power house of Dinorwig Power Plant have been built deep inside the mountain.

When demand for electricity is high, water rushes down through the tunnels and makes the turbines spin very rapidly.

At night, the turbines are put into reverse. They pump water out of the lower reservoir and up into the upper reservoir. This job can take as long as six hours. There, the water is stored for the next peak in demand.

▲ Dinorwig Power Plant in North Wales. When the power plant was designed, a great effort was made not to spoil the countryside. Because of this effort, the completed power plant is hidden from view. The upper reservoir is on the left of the picture. Can you see where the water enters the lower reservoir?

Water Power

In some hydroelectric power systems, engineers use electricity to pump water up to a high reservoir late at night. This is when the demand for electricity is at its lowest. When the demand is high, the pumped water is brought down through tubes to the power plant to turn the turbines. This is called a **pumped storage system**.

The hydroelectric power plants which use the force of the Niagara River in the United States and Canada also use the pumped storage system. During the night, water is pumped up into the reservoir above the Robert Moses Power Plant. The same thing happens at the Sir Adam Beck Power Plant on the Canadian side of the river.

Both these power plants use their stored river water to generate electricity during the peak periods throughout the day.

Using River Power

The world's rivers release a huge amount of power in the form of kinetic energy as they flow back to the sea. So far, only a small part of this energy is used to produce power that we can use.

Small Systems

Many countries have long, fast-flowing rivers passing through them. These rivers contain so much energy that they could be used over and over again to make electricity. Much of this water power could be used if small power plants were built along the river. Electricity can be generated even if the water level drops by only three feet. The author Rudyard Kipling used a small stream in his garden in England to make hydroelectricity over eight years ago. He used this power to light up his home.

The Chinese have built 90,000 small power plants along their rivers. This provides much of the electricity that China needs. Small power plants are often cheap to build and run.

▲ Farmers in Southeast Asia often use rivers to flood their fields on purpose. These farmers are planting rice seedlings in the water of the rice paddies.

▼ These water mills are anchored in the Danube River in Yugoslavia. The current of the river turns the wheels.

Floods

The energy and power of a big river can be seen when it floods. Floods often cause damage, but they can be helpful as well. The Nile River used to flood its banks each year. It left rich mud on the banks when the water went down. The farmers of Egypt stored the flood water to water their crops. This is called **irrigation**. Now, the Aswan High Dam controls the Nile River. The dam provides water for Egypt and its neighbor, Sudan, when it is needed, not just once a year.

Dams to keep back flood water have been built along the Tennessee River and its side valleys. The water is used to produce hydroelectricity and also for irrigation. If it is controlled, the power of a flooding river can benefit, rather than harm, the people who live along its banks.

▼ You can see how much energy there is in a river. Flooding rivers can cause enormous damage. When they break their banks, they often wash away trees, roads, bridges, and buildings.

Using the Tides

The place where the river empties into the sea is called its **estuary**. Most river estuaries are tidal. Salt water in the sea moves up the river at high tide. About six hours later, at low tide, the salt water flows back into the sea.

Tides

The pull of the sun and moon causes the movement of the tides. In some places, the difference in height between high and low tide is only about three feet. It depends on the shape of the coast and on the ocean currents. The greatest difference in the rise and fall of the tide can be seen at the Bay of Fundy in Canada. There, the difference in height is over forty-eight feet.

Tide Mills

Tides are a source of energy. People in northern France used tidal mills with water wheels over 900 years ago. Today, engineers are looking at new ways of using tidal power.

The machinery used in the old tidal mills was like that of a water mill. At high tide, the incoming sea water went through sluice gates into a millpond. The sluice gates shut tightly when the tide turned and the level of the water started to drop. The pond was then much higher than the level of the rest of the water in the estuary. The miller released the sea water from the pond at low tide. As the water rushed back to the sea from the pond, it turned a water wheel which was used to grind corn.

◄ Four hundred years ago, there were tide mills along the estuaries of many rivers in Britain and France. The white building is the tide mill at Woodbridge in England, at low tide.

► The dam across the Rance River in Brittany, France. Its twenty-four turbines are turned one way by the incoming tide. A few hours later, they are turned the other way by the outgoing tide.

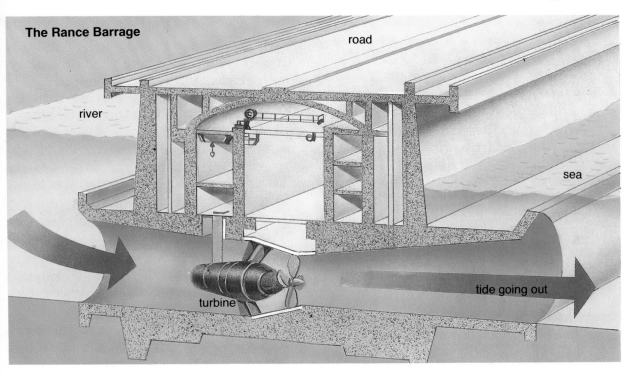

The Rance Barrage

road

river

sea

tide going out

turbine

Tidal Power Plants

Tidal power plants are in use in France and in the USSR. The Rance **Barrage** in France was built over twenty years ago. It uses the tides of the Rance River estuary to make electricity. At high tide, the river level is twenty-six feet above the level at low tide. As the level rises, the water turns the turbines in the Rance power plant. When the tide goes out, the water turns the turbines the other way. The power plant makes enough electricity to supply an area the size of a large city. Why are there not more tidal power plants? The water power does exist. A huge tidal wave, called the "Severn Bore," enters the Severn River estuary in Britain. Experts say it could make thirty times as much electricity as the Rance power plant. The main problem is that tidal power plants are difficult and expensive to build. A plan to build a tidal power plant in the Bay of Fundy in Canada failed. The cost of building a dam there was too expensive. Extra-strong dam walls would have been needed there, because the tides are so strong. Tidal power plants have other disadvantages. They can produce electricity only for a few hours each day. Half of this power is produced at night when there is not much need for extra electricity.

Wave Power

Nearly three quarters of the earth's surface is covered by water. Most of this is salt water. Scientists think it could provide us with energy in the future. It would be very useful because the surface of the ocean is seldom still. Currents move large quantities of water from one part of the ocean to another. Waves up to eighty feet in height are formed. The force of these waves could become a valuable source of energy, if we knew how to control it.

The Power of the Waves

Waves are formed by the wind. The strongest winds are those which blow over long stretches of the sea or the ocean. The strongest winds form crests of waves which are called **swells**. The longer and stronger the wind blows, the bigger the waves are. Power made with these waves would help to meet the peak demand for electricity. This is because strong winds often bring bad weather. People use more electricity when the weather is bad.

▼ Waves damage the coast. They cut caves in cliffs and wash away beaches. Sometimes, they destroy piers and sea walls, as in this picture.

▲ As water and air enter the sea clams system, the energy of the waves is converted into electricity. It could be used to provide power for people on remote islands.

Using the Waves

Engineers have invented many methods for using wave power, but not many have been tried out yet. Scientists are still working on them. Professor Stephen Salter at Edinburgh University has invented one method. It uses machines which float on the sea. The machine has flaps which are joined to a long central column, or shaft. The flaps move up and down as the waves pass them. They move a turbine which makes electricity. The flaps look like bobbing ducks, so the method is called the Salter Ducks.

Another method was invented by Sir Christopher Cockerell. The Cockerell Rafts are hinged in the middle. They flap up and down with the waves and force water through pumps. A third method would use huge plastic bags. The waves would squash the air in the bags, and then the air would drive a turbine. All these machines would be anchored to the sea bed.

Scientists in Norway have been working on two other methods for using wave power. The first wave power plant was opened in Norway in 1985. Engineers built a tower, or column, in the sea cliffs near Bergen. The column is sixty-five feet high, and it is hollow. Waves rush in and out of the column. They push air in the tower upward. The air falls back as the water flows out of the column. As the air moves up and down, it turns a special turbine. This method is called the Oscillating Water Column.

The second method used in Norway is called Tapchan. Waves flow fast along a narrow concrete channel in the cliffs. They spill over into a reservoir. From there, the water flows through pipes to power a turbine.

Both of these methods were built with the help of Professor Salter and the people working for him. The methods used in Norway make electricity more cheaply than some power plants which use coal and nuclear energy.

Many other machines are being designed, but these are the only two which have been built.

Using the Wind

There is a new interest in windmills. This is because most people know that the world's fossil fuels, such as coal, oil, and natural gas, will run out someday. As they become scarce, the price of fuel will rise. Wind, like water in the sea, is free. It will not run out.

Windpumps

Sixty years ago, there were over five million windpumps on the farms of the American West. Many are still used today

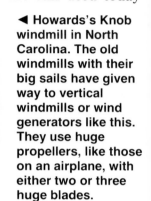

◄ Howards's Knob windmill in North Carolina. The old windmills with their big sails have given way to vertical windmills or wind generators like this. They use huge propellers, like those on an airplane, with either two or three huge blades.

► Wind farms have to be built in places where there are high, nearly-constant wind speeds and plenty of space. This wind farm is at Altamount in California.

for pumping water. The windpumps are metal towers which stand over a well. At the top of the towers are metal wheels. Each wheel has about twenty blades. When the wind blows, the wheels spin around and raise water from the well into a storage tank. The water is used for crops and animals, as well as by the household.

In the 1930s, many wind generators were also built in North America. They made enough electricity to supply a single farm. They were simple to use and seldom broke down. Wind generators are still used in many parts of the world where a small, local supply of electricity is needed.

The World's Largest Windmill

In 1979, the world's largest windmill was built at Howard's Knob in North Carolina. It has blades instead of sails. The blades are 195 feet in length. This windmill generates enough electricity to supply a small town of about 500 homes. About 1,000 similar windmills would be needed to replace a single power plant which burns coal or oil. One thousand giant windmills would take up a lot of space.

Wind Farms

When groups of wind generators are built close to each other, we call them a "wind farm." Wind farms have been built to provide electricity in California. A similar wind farm is planned for the Isle of Man in Britain. Wind farms have to be built in places where it is very windy. This is not always close to the places where the most people live, so electricity has to be carried to the towns. High towers are needed to make the best use of the winds. Giant wind generators can be dangerous. Blades can snap off in a gale. Also, they are very noisy. There is a constant whirring and swishing from the huge blades. Very few people would want to live close to a wind farm.

Building wind farms out at sea could be the answer. There are no hills, buildings, or trees out at sea to keep the wind from reaching the generators. The noise of the whirring blades would not annoy anyone, although the towers would spoil the look of the sea. They might also be dangerous to ships at night or in a fog. They might also affect such wildlife as birds and fish.

Changing Energy

Energy cannot be made or destroyed. It can be changed from one form to another, or moved from one place to another. For thousands of years, different ways of changing and using the sun's energy have been tried. People have wanted to change energy to make their lives easier.

Food and Animals

Our own energy comes from the food we eat. It is one of the main ways in which we make use of the sun's energy. Sunlight helps plants to grow. The plants store the sun's energy. They make a substance called **carbohydrates**. This is why carbohydrates are found in many of the foods we eat,

such as cereals. It is a good source of energy for people, too.

Carbohydrates are also found in food for animals. Stored energy passes from plants to animals when horses eat oats or barley. The horses store this energy for future use, so it can be used to move their muscles. They change the stored energy in food into **mechanical energy** when they use their muscles to pull a cart or plow.

The horse was the main source of power before the steam engine. This is why energy was once measured in **horsepower**. A ten-horsepower car did as much work as ten horses.

▼ Horses were more common than tractors on Europe's farms until about 1950. Cattle, horses, camels, llamas, and other animals still do much of the hard work on some of the world's farms. Some of the stored energy in this crop is being eaten by the horse, so he will have enough energy to pull the heavy cart.

Energy from Wind and Water

We also change energy from one form to another at a hydroelectric power plant. The kinetic energy of moving water turns the water turbines to make electrical energy.

Sails change the kinetic energy of the wind into mechanical energy when a sail boat moves through the water. Sailing ships sometimes took a hundred days to cross the Atlantic Ocean from Europe to North America. Later, steamships made the same journey in less than four days, but only after burning a large amount of fuel. In the future, we may see many more ships with sails as well as engines. The ships would not go so fast, but they would not use as much **nonrenewable** energy, either.

Heat from the Sea

Energy has also been changed from one form to another in the Ocean Thermal Energy Converters (OTEC). The OTEC system has been tested in warm, tropical seas. The system has been built to make use of the difference in heat between the surface of the sea and the water ninety-eight feet below the surface. This difference can measure as much as 27°F to 36°F.

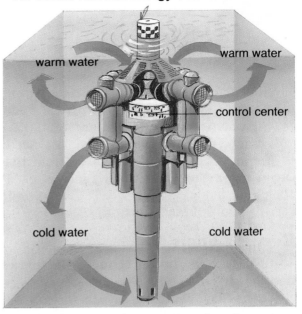

An Ocean Thermal Energy Converter

warm water

warm water

control center

cold water

cold water

OTECs use the energy in the warm water at the ocean surface to boil a liquid, such as ammonia. This liquid has a much lower boiling point than water, so less heat is needed to make it boil. The gas given off by the boiling ammonia drives a gas turbine which makes electricity. Water from the ocean depths cools these gases once they have been used. This turns them back into liquid to start the process all over again.

► Ships like this one, with sails controlled by computers, save fuel. They take longer to make a voyage, but they can save thousands of tons of oil a year.

Looking Ahead

What will happen to the world's supply of energy? This question worries many people. Some people are afraid that there will not be enough energy for all our needs in the future. Other people are afraid that the way we burn our fossil fuels, such as coal, oil, and natural gas, will damage the earth's atmosphere.

Burning Fuels

Burning coal and oil changes the air we breathe. It sends tons of chemicals into the air each day. Sometimes, factories spill waste chemicals into the rivers or into the air. Traffic also gives off gases which can poison the air. This is called **pollution**. Scientists think that pollution may be the reason why many trees have died in North America and Europe. It may also be the reason why some rivers and lakes have no fish in them now. Power plants which burn coal are blamed for much of the world's air pollution problem.

The main offenders are the industrial countries. They use most of the world's coal, oil, and natural gas. These fossil fuels still supply about ninety percent of the energy we use. This is nonrenewable

▲ This wind generator is in Spain. In the future, we may see more generators like this all over the world.

◄ In some parts of the world, hot water bubbles to the surface. At this geothermal power plant in Australia, the water is used to generate electricity. Scientists are looking for other ways to use the heat inside the earth.

energy. Pollution will still be a problem when the world's supplies of oil and natural gas are all gone. This is because large supplies of coal are still untouched. More coal will be burned in the future, unless new sources of energy are developed first. When all the coal, as well as the oil and natural gas, is gone, the people of the future will have to use other types of energy. They will have no other choice.

Wasting Energy

We waste a great deal of the energy we produce. The demand for more coal, oil, and natural gas continues to grow. If people stopped wasting energy, the demand for fuel would fall.

Huge amounts of heat escape into the atmosphere each year through walls, windows, roofs, and chimneys. We throw away many "waste" products. Some paper, metals, and glass can be used again. This is called **recycling**. Furnaces have already been built to burn garbage to make

electricity. Taking greater care of sources of energy like this is called **conservation**.

Mixed Energy

Wind power and water power on their own cannot supply all the energy which will be needed in the future. The best use for wind power and water power will be to help make the world's supplies of coal, oil, and natural gas last longer.

The main advantages of wind power and water power are that they are renewable. They are also cheap to run and sometimes cheaper to build than other kinds of power plants. They do not pollute the air. Wind farms may soon be a familiar sight on hills or at sea. Tidal power plants and wave power plants may be built around the coasts. In the future, we will probably know about many more ways of using the sun's energy than we do today.

Winds, rivers, waves, and tides may all help to provide the world with the energy it needs.

In the future the world may use all these different sources of energy.

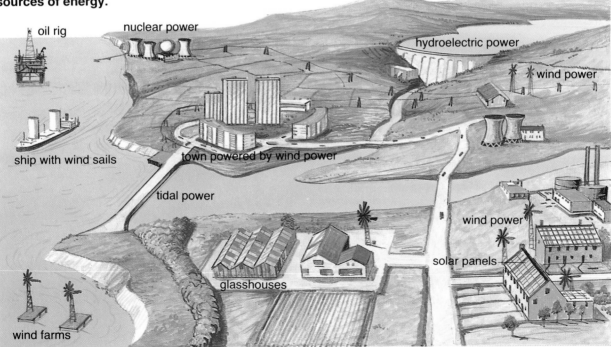

oil rig · nuclear power · hydroelectric power · wind power · ship with wind sails · town powered by wind power · tidal power · wind power · solar panels · glasshouses · wind farms

Glossary

air pressure: the layers of air pressing down on the earth. The greatest pressure is felt at ground level. The higher up you go, the less air there is and the lower the air pressure becomes.

aqueduct: a channel built to carry water across a valley or through an underground tunnel. The first aqueducts were built by the Romans and were made of stone or brick.

atmosphere: the layer of gases that surrounds a planet. The earth's atmosphere is the air. It is made up of several gases.

barrage: an artificial bar across a river.

base load: the lowest amount of electricity that power plants can expect to supply each day throughout the year.

breastshot: a mill wheel which is turned by water pushing it in the middle.

buttress dam: a type of dam where there is extra strength in the blocks of concrete, or buttresses, built at the front of the dam wall.

carbohydrate: an energy-giving substance made by green plants.

chemical: any substance which can change when joined or mixed with another substance.

chemical energy: energy made by a chemical reaction. This may happen when two substances mix.

compressed air: air squeezed into a container, so that its pressure is higher than the air outside.

conduct: to guide or channel something along a particular path. Electricity is conducted easily along copper wire.

conservation: the protection and careful use of something. The protection of the countryside, fuel, wildlife, or old buildings is called conservation.

electric current: a flow of electricity.

electrical energy: a kind of energy or power which can travel along wires. It is used to heat and light homes and to run many machines.

electron: a tiny particle of electricity which is found in all atoms. It carries a negative charge.

energy: the power to do work. People get energy from food. Engines get energy from fuel like gasoline.

equator: an imaginary line around the middle of the earth. The hottest parts of the world are nearest to the equator.

estuary: the wide mouth of a river where it meets the sea.

evaporate: to change from a liquid into a gas. Heat from the sun makes water evaporate into the air.

force of gravity: the force that pulls everything toward the center of a planet. Gravity makes objects fall and gives them weight.

fossil fuel: the remains of animals and plants which lived millions of years ago which we use for fuel. Coal and oil are fossil fuels.

generate: to make or create something.

generator: a machine for changing mechanical energy into electrical energy.

geothermal energy: a type of energy produced by using the heat from below the earth's surface.

head of water: a way of measuring the force of water at a dam or waterfall.

headrace: the channel or chute which takes water from a river or lake to a water wheel.

high pressure: describes the air pressure near the earth when it is being pushed down more strongly than usual.

horizontal mill: a windmill in which the sails turn around level with, or parallel to, the ground.

horsepower: a measurement of power. It is used because in the past people compared the power of a machine with the amount of work a single horse could do.

hydroelectric power: electricity which has been made by using fast-flowing water to drive a turbine.

industry: the work which makes or produces goods, often in a factory.

irrigation: watering land that has too little rain by using a system of pipes and ditches. The water is pumped from rivers, lakes, or from under the ground. Irrigation makes it possible to grow crops in the desert.

kinetic energy: the energy in something when it moves.

leat: a channel taking water to a water wheel.

low pressure: describes the air pressure near the earth when it is being pushed down less strongly than usual.

magnetism: having the power to attract.

mechanical energy: energy which is used to do a job, such as by a person, by a machine, or by an animal.

millstone: a flat, round stone used for crushing grain into flour.

natural gas: a gas often found close to oil. Most of it is methane gas.

nonrenewable: describes something which cannot be replaced.

nuclear energy: the power produced by the heat made when atoms are split.

ocean current: the steady flow in one direction of a large amount of water in an ocean.

overshot: a mill wheel which is turned by water pushing from above.

peak load: the highest amount of electricity that power plants have to be able to supply. A peak load happens when there is a sudden demand for power.

penstock: the gate or channel controlling a flow of water.

Persia: a country now called Iran. It was once an ancient empire which stretched from Egypt to India.

pollution: something which dirties or poisons the air, land, or water. Wastes from factories cause pollution.

post mill: a wooden windmill built on a thick post. The mill could be turned on this post so that the sails could face the wind.

potential energy: energy which is stored to be ready for use at a later time.

power line: a wire cable carrying electricity.

proton: a tiny particle of electricity which is found in all atoms. It has a positive charge.

pumped storage system: a system which uses cheap, plentiful electricity at night, to pump water to a higher level. The water is then reused to make hydroelectricity during the day when there is a much greater demand for electric power.

pylon: a tall steel frame or column for supporting power lines above the ground.

recycling: to use a waste material again. Paper, metals, and glass can all be recycled.

renewable: that which can be replaced, or made new again.

reservoir: a very large tank or lake where water is collected and stored.

rotation: the turning or spinning of a planet on its axis.

shaft: a rod which is used to carry or pull something along. In an engine, a metal rod carries the power from the engine to the wheels.

sluice gate: a gate in a waterway which is used to change the flow of water. It can be opened to different degrees in order to control the amount of water going through, or closed completely to keep the water back.

smock mill: another name for a tower mill. Only the cap of the windmill turns around to face the wind.

solar energy: energy from the sun's rays. Solar energy can be used to make electricity.

spillway: a channel that takes water away from a dam after it has been used.

static electricity: an electric charge produced by rubbing.

swell: regular up and down movement of the sea.

tailrace: the channel or chute taking water away from a water wheel after it has been used.

tower mill: a tall windmill. Only the very top of the windmill turns around to face the wind.

transformer: a machine which changes the force of an electric current.

troposphere: the layer of air about eight miles thick just above the surface of the earth. It is named after two Greek words meaning "movement" (tropos) and "ball" (sphere). The troposphere is thicker at the equator than at the two Poles.

turbine: a wheel which has many curved blades. It is spun around rapidly by the movement of a gas or a liquid. Turbines drive machines which make electricity.

undershot: a mill wheel which is turned by water pushing from below.

vane: a flat or curved blade. It can be set to direct the flow of air or a liquid, or be free to move to produce power or show a direction.

vertical: upright. When people stand up straight, they are in a vertical position.

vertical mill: a windmill in which the sails turn around at right angles to the ground.

volt: a measurement of the force of an electric current.

water cycle: the movement of water from the air to the ground and sea and back again to the air.

water vapor: water as a gas.

weir: a low dam built across a river. Water flows over the top of the weir when the river is full.

wind current: a flow of a large amount of air in one direction.

Index